Dear Parents,

Congratulations for choosing a fun and entertaining way to help your child learn to interact with others in pleasing, socially acceptable ways!

Children have the ability to be good, and they are often eager to please. However, they often don't understand their own egocentric or self-centered behavior. This self-centeredness often leads to misbehavior, and the misbehavior often leads to negative responses from others. All too soon, your child can be caught in a destructive cycle of negative action and reaction.

The purpose of the HELP ME BE GOOD books is to help your child break the cycle of negative action and reaction. Your child will learn how to replace misbehavior with acceptable behavior. Each HELP ME BE GOOD book is designed to do the following in an enjoyable way:

1. Define a misbehavior
2. Explain the cause of the misbehavior
3. Discuss the negative effects of the misbehavior
4. Offer suggestions for replacing the misbehavior with acceptable behavior

While it is effective to read the individual HELP ME BE GOOD books when a need arises, the series was designed to follow the normal development of young children. Consequently, presenting the books to your child in the order in which they are listed on the back cover of this book also works well.

As you and your child read the HELP ME BE GOOD books, your child will develop good behavior that will help build positive self-esteem and healthy relationships. Reading the books will also help to create a more friendly, happy atmosphere in your home. Thank you for allowing me to be a part of this exciting endeavor!

Sincerely,

Joy Berry

Joy Berry

Copyright© Joy Berry, 2022
Originally Published, 2008

All rights are reserved.

No part of this book can be duplicated or used without the prior written permission of the copyright owner, except for the use of brief quotations from the book.

For inquiries or permission requests contact the publisher.

Published by Joy Berry Enterprises
www.joyberryenterprises.com

A Help Me Be Good Book About

Stealing

Written By Joy Berry
Illustrated By Bartholomew

Copyright © 2008 by Joy Berry

This book is about Karen and her friend Lennie.

Reading about Karen and Lennie can help you understand and deal with **stealing.**

Has anyone ever taken something that belonged to you and not returned it?

You are stealing when you take and keep something that does not belong to you.

If someone steals from you:
- You might feel disappointed, frustrated, and angry.
- You might think that the person cannot be trusted.
- You might not want that person to be near your things.

It is important to treat other people the way you want to be treated.

If you do not want other people to steal from you, you must not steal from them.

Sometimes you might take something *by accident.*

You might borrow something and forget to return it.

You might take something without thinking about it.

The things you take accidentally need to be returned right away.

Sometimes people take things *on purpose*. They know what they are doing. They choose to steal.

Sometimes people steal *because they want something or because they think they need something*. They might think that they cannot be happy unless they have the thing they are stealing.

Sometimes people steal *because their friends steal.*

They might think it is OK to steal because their friends do it.

They might not want to be different from their friends who steal.

They might think their friends will like them better if they steal.

Sometimes people steal *because they think what they do will not make a difference.* They think no one will notice. They tell themselves their stealing will not hurt anyone.

Sometimes people steal *because they are angry.* They want to get back at someone who has done something to hurt them.

Stealing is wrong. No matter why people do it, it is never OK to take something that does not belong to you.

Try to make things right if you have stolen anything. Return what you have stolen if it is not broken or ruined.

If it is broken or ruined, replace it or pay for it.

Tell the person you stole from that you are sorry. Then do not steal again.

It is important to treat other people the way you want to be treated.

If you do not want other people to steal from you, you must not steal from them.

Stealing Song Lyrics
Music & Lyrics by Joy Berry, Shanin Jones & Rita Abrams

Stealing

A kid, Mike,
Stole my bike.
From then on,
It was gone.
I told my dad.
He got mad.
Then I cried.
I thought I'd die.

Stealing is taking things
That don't belong to you.
Stealing is taking things,
And it's against the rules.

A kid, Paul,
Stole my ball,
Took it home
On his own.
I told mom
It was gone.
She got mad.
I felt bad.

Stealing is taking things
That don't belong to you.
Stealing is taking things,
And it's against the rules.

My friend, Roy,
Took my toy,
Brought it back,
I like that.
He was fair,
And he cared.
In the end,
We stayed friends.

Stealing is taking things
That don't belong to you.
Stealing is taking things,
And it's against the rules.

Stealing is taking things
That don't belong to you.
Stealing is taking things,
And it's against the rules.

You Don't Really Want to Steal

Gee, I've always wanted one of those.
Wonder if I took it, who would know?

Put those things behind,
And make up your mind.
You don't really want to steal.

Gee, but this is just what I've been needing.
Wonder if I took it, who would see me?

Put those thoughts away,
'Cause it's safe to say,
You don't really want to steal.

Maybe 'cause you want it.
Maybe 'cause your friends do.
Maybe 'cause you're angry
At someone who hurt you.

Doesn't matter why.
Doesn't matter who.
Stealing is just never right to do.

Feeling better now that I can see,
Stealing never will be right for me.

Glad you made it through.
Glad it dawned on you,
You don't really want to steal,
You don't really want to steal.

Visit us on the web at www.joyberryenterprises.com!

www.ingramcontent.com/pod-product-compliance
Lightning Source LLC
Chambersburg PA
CBHW081411070526
44583CB00020B/2762